What they don't tell you about University

Myths Explained. Experiences Shared. Success Guaranteed.

CRYSTAL DEBRAH

DS Publishers
Publish.Market.Sell

For permission request, contact the publisher
at the email address below:
Email: info@sdpublishers.com
Website: www.sdpublishers.com

Author: Crystal Debrah
Publisher: SDPublishers
Cover Design: Ibiere Oruwari
Typeset: MaestroCreativity
Distributed by SDPublishers

Paperback ISBN: 978-0-9568028-0-4

This publication is designed to provide accurate and authoritative information in regard to the subject matter covered. It is sold with the understanding that neither the author nor the publisher is engaged in rendering legal, accounting, or other professional service.

If legal advice or other expert assistance is required, the services of a competent professional should be sought.

Note: The material contained in this book is set out in good faith for general guidance and no liability can be accepted for loss or expense incurred as a result of relying in particular circumstances on statements made in the book.

Dedication

Dedicated to my parents
Stanley and Gladys Debrah.

Acknowledgement

I would like to thank the Lord for giving me the ability to write this book.

I would like to thank my parents, my sister Helen Debrah, Yinka Soname, Kunle Oyedeji, Remi Banjo, Iyabo Eferakoro, Sandra Wheeler, Ebun Abatan, Jide Fisher, Zainab Adamu, Rebecca Palmer and the Peer Outreach Team for their support and encouragement. I would also like to thank Ibiere Oruwari for designing the book and SDPublishers for publishing my book.. I would also like to thank all those I interviewed.

To those whose names may not be mentioned, you are not forgotten.

"With tuition fees set to rise it is essential for young people to go to university knowing what to expect and how to get the most for their money. This book covers the essentials in a clear, coherent and practical way. If you're thinking about whether or not to go to university or want an understanding of how it all works then this short, yet informative guide is for you. I've read it and think it is brilliant, what a great idea. Crystal is definitely one to watch."

**Rebecca Palmer, Greater London Authority,
City Hall**

"There is a saying that if you fail to prepare then you are preparing to fail. This book gives every student the opportunity to get a head start and is everything a student needs to prepare themselves for success in education. A must read and certainly a recommendation of mine."

Kunlé Oyedeji, Director of Life Solutions

"This book helped to calm my nerves and acts as a helpful guideline."

Alan Omogbai, Fresher

"The book is clear, succinct, and very to the point. Students need this book as one can quickly find vital information about university life."

Esther Adeyi, Fresher

"The book is really helpful, especially the advice about the study techniques. I have got a better idea of how to tackle my subject despite having completed one degree."

Jason Rowe, Postgraduate Student

"I am 18 and employed. I would definitely buy this book if I went to university as it seems very helpful."

Peer Outreach Worker,

Children and Young Persons' Unit

Preface

This book was written during my second and third years of university. I struggled to get to grips with university life and ended first year with a 3rd class grade. I approached lecturers and fellow students in order to find out how to improve.

I utilised all the information I was given and completed my degree with a 2:1 grade. I've placed all this information into a simple guide to ensure new undergraduates know what to expect and can therefore excel from the outset. I wish I had known this information before going to university.

Use this guide as a reference book throughout your studies.

Good luck!

Contents

1
Introduction

Congratulations! Going to university is another step on the ladder of education; however time will seem to go by quicker than expected. This book is designed to assist you in making your time at university as productive as possible.

Before going any further, it is important to take a moment to consider what you think university would be like. While going through this book many expectations may be met and some may even be challenged.

10 Reasons to go to University

1. Investment in your future. Those competing with you for jobs are likely to have degrees.

2. Higher earning capacity upon graduation.

3. Meet other future professionals and create good networks for the future.

4. Make friends for life.

5. Learn to look after yourself away from home.

6. Experience new activities and cultures.

7. Connect to influential lecturers.

8. A chance to challenge yourself to reach your full potential.

9. Work hard and play hard.

10. Acquire more knowledge.

The Truth

University could be seen as a place to discover your strengths and weaknesses; a place where you meet some of your closest friends, as well as a place to "discover yourself". Whatever the duration of the degree, the key is to use your time effectively; this is done by doing as much as possible in the time that is given. This applies to your academic, extra-curricular and social life.

Myths about University Life

1. "First year does not count."

This is not necessarily true! There are numerous recruiters for work experience or internships that may ask for the grades attained in the first year of your course, so it may be best to attain a 1st or a 2:1 grade.

Moreover, doing well in your first year will give you confidence and motivation for the following academic year.

2. "University is all about independent work."

In many courses much of the work is independent; however it is possible to ask for help. Most lecturers have "office hours". These are time slots where an individual lecturer will be available for consultation about the course. It is strongly recommend that a list be made of all relevant lecturers and seminar teachers' office hours within the first month of the degree. Do not be shy in approaching them as they want you to do well on the course.

3. "Students go out every night."

First year students from any discipline are notorious for staggering back to their campus rooms after a late night out. What many people forget is that they are in university to LEARN. Do have fun, do go out, but please be mindful of the workload that is given and how much time may be needed to do the work properly. In other words, time needs to be balanced effectively (this will be discussed later).

2
How to Make Friends

S ome people can approach anyone and start a conversation, while others are not as confident. Universities create opportunities to make new friends so take full advantage of them.

Freshers' Week (s)

It is possible that by now the university may have already started to send leaflets about "Freshers' Week". This is where parties and socials are promoted. On my "Freshers' Week" there was a social/party everyday and it was a great chance for me to meet new people. Remember, you will not meet people if you do not put yourself out there. Think of it this way, everybody is new and possibly a little nervous!

Also all the student societies market their activities, for example, the basketball team, the fashion society or a charitable society. There are many societies, these range from sport to debating. Consider trying something new. Joining societies is one of the most effective ways of meeting people, so it is recommended to join at least one society.

Advice

If choosing societies becomes difficult, choose activities which will develop and enhance career prospects. These do not have to be related to the degree that is being studied.

More Advice

It may also be a good idea to volunteer while studying as volunteering is looked upon favourably by employers. Academics are very important; however work experience is also very important.

3
How to Get the Most Out of Your Degree
"Monitor your Attitude and Resources"

Your Attitude

The attitude you adopt is the most important key to success if you want to achieve a good grade at degree level.

"Nothing can stop the man with the right mental attitude from achieving his goal; nothing on earth can help the man with the wrong mental attitude." - Thomas Jefferson

University is very different from sixth form/college. How much or how little time you spend studying is up to you. The lecturers, unlike teachers, will not compel anyone to study. This means that you have to schedule your time and motivate yourself. Here are two ways in which you can.

1. Plan your time

Once the academic timetable has been received, it would be best to plan the time effectively. Below is an example of a university timetable.

	MON	TUES	WED
9:00am			
10:00am			
11:00am			
12:00pm	Subsidiary Module (British Sign Language)		
1:00pm	Subsidiary Module (British Sign Language)	Cognitive Psychology	
2:00pm	Subsidiary Module (British Sign Language)	Cognitive Psychology	Basketball
3:00pm			
4:00pm		Statistics	
5:00pm		Statistics	
6:00pm	Look over past exam papers		

THU	FRI	SAT	SUN
	Cognitive Neuroscience & biological psychology	Part time job	
Practical Methods	Cognitive Neuroscience & biological psychology		
Practical Methods	Subsidiary seminar (Philosophy)		
Practical Methods			Volunteer work at the shelter
Seminar (every other week)	Individual in Society		
	Individual in Society		
			Seminar Preparation
	Relax		

Advice for effective time management

a. Realistically discover how much time will be needed to prepare for each module. This can be done by allocating the amount of time you think you will need. Place it into the appropriate place on a timetable.

b. Test it out for the week and make adjustments where necessary. For example, give yourself less time to complete the work.

c. Ensure some time to relax and have fun is included!

d. Stick to the timetable! This can easily become a routine, which will make study time much easier.

2. Be positive

During the first year of the course the workload may seem to be vast. I for one thought about quitting my law degree because of the volume of work, but did not. It may get tough but remember, passing the course is achievable and you can do it. I did not understand this truth until my second year of university and it helped me to keep the momentum going all academic year. You cannot go beyond what you think, so picture yourself receiving that first class degree and do the necessary work required to achieve it. You are a product of your thinking.

Your Resources

1. Reading materials

For every course a "reading list" will be given that contains specific books for each module. Some students utilise the books on loan in the university library and continue renewing it throughout the entire year without purchasing textbooks. This is not recommended if the book is in high demand because there may be limited access to it. It is best to purchase books first or second hand depending on your financial situation. It is likely that second year students will approach new students with books needed for the first year so the required books can be purchased from them. However, this must be done with caution as textbooks are often updated on a yearly basis. Seek advice from lecturers and seminar teachers before purchasing books from students.

When reading the materials, be sure to cover what is required by using lecture handouts and seminar questions as a guide to what is important. Any extra information that may be acquired is a bonus. Examinations will be based on how well the relevant material is known. Make an effort in class assessments as these will give an indication of what improvements need to be made, even if the assessments do not contribute to the final grade.

2. Lecturers and seminar teachers

Aside from the prescribed material, seminar teachers and lecturers are very important. Unlike school, the lecturers write the examination papers. With this in mind, it is sensible to visit them during their office hours and ask them questions about difficulties that may be faced. During these conversations they are likely to drop hints (whether they know it or not) about the most important issues and how to approach them in an exam or essay. I personally approached all my lecturers and visited them on at least three occasions during the academic year. In doing this I could understand the relevant material; I was able to discover whether or not my own ideas made sense and I established relationships with each lecturer (this is valuable for future job application references also).

Take notes when speaking to lecturers and seminar teachers. Advice and guidance given by them can be noted during or after a conversation. This will be valuable when it comes to revision time. It is also recommended that their email addresses are obtained for important questions on a particular subject that may arise during the course.

3. Other students

Studying alone may be frustrating if the material that has been given is not understood. It is recommended that no more than three other

people meet and discuss the material. If the group is too large it will be difficult to focus. This could be due to the fact that people may contribute too many ideas resulting in not enough time being set aside/ left to understand the core material.

4. Past exam papers

At some universities past exam papers can be found on the university website or in the library. If they are not easily accessible ask a personal tutor for help in obtaining them.

Approximately one month into the course, obtain past exam papers. This is recommended as it will give an idea of what is to be expected for the examinations. It is best to thoroughly revise them.

- Do not worry if the papers are not initially understood because all the material will not have been covered by this stage.
- Look at these papers as often as possible during the year. My lecturer advised me to do this fortnightly for the sake of familiarity.
- The more the papers are looked at, the more comfortable it will be tackling them.
- Look for similarities in the papers. However, this must be done with caution, as a new lecturer may be setting your paper.

- Write down questions to ask lecturers/seminar teachers regarding the exam papers and visit or email them when possible. Keep their answers safe for the exam period.
- Consider how to tackle the questions.
- Discuss the papers with friends.

4
Study Techniques

"Do what works for you"

Completing the Reading

Many of the humanities subjects may require further reading over and above the prescribed reading.

- Tackle the essential reading first and once it is understood move onto further reading. If this is not covered in time there is no need to panic, there is still an opportunity to read the further reading during the exam period.
- As previously mentioned, use lecture notes and seminar materials as a guide.
- Doing extra research on what interests you could be beneficial. If this research can be put into an examination essay answer you will obtain higher marks. So ensure that research is relevant.

Which Method of Study Suits You?

I have noticed from my time at university that a number of students only write linear notes. This is fine if this is how you have mastered how to study. However, this is not advised if you do not effectively learn this way.

Think about the learning style you have used in the past and integrate this way of learning into studying your degree.

Available Study Techniques

These techniques can be utilised during the year and for revision time.

- Mind maps

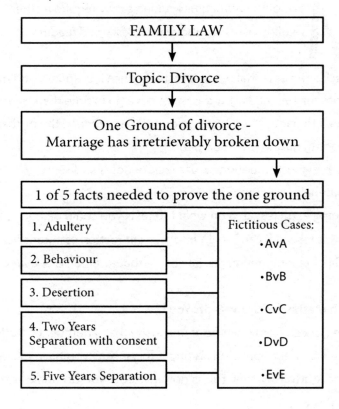

- Explain what has been learnt to someone on your course.
- Explain what has been learnt to someone not studying the same course. If what is explained has been fully understood, it is a sign that you understand the material well.
- Listen to recorded lectures (be sure to ask the lecturer for permission before recording lectures).
- Listen to podcasts or watch lecture videos.
- Write notes using different colours.
- Spider diagrams may be useful.
- Re-write notes and condense them.

Feel free in experimenting with these techniques and discover which are best suited. The list above is not exhaustive and other methods which were not mentioned above can be discovered.

5
What Lecturers Want

What is expected from candidates?

1. Essays
2. Independent learning
3. Time management skills
4. Reading and thinking beyond the immediate subject matter of your course
5. Research skills
6. Use of accredited information
7. Clarity of expression (verbal and written)
8. Prioritising
9. Understanding

Most Frequent Mistakes

1. Preparing for exams

a. Students often only revise a certain number of topics and ignore others. For example, the exam may require students to answer four questions out of a possible seven; some students will only revise four topics. DO NOT DO THIS. It is good to focus on your best topics but overall knowledge will enhance the answers that are given.

b. Often students spend too much time learning and memorising, and not enough time evaluating information given to them.

c. Be aware of what is in the news regarding your subject. Such information can be used as an example to support exam answers. Lecturers may also be impressed by this.

2. In exams

a.   Answer the correct number of questions.

b.   Plan your time.

3. General preparation

a. Naturally build knowledge to add to general knowledge (for example, read newspapers).

b.   Discuss material with friends.

The Use of Lectures and Seminars

1. Lectures

a.   It is advised that lecture materials and prescribed reading are read ahead of lectures for better understanding of what is being presented.

b.   Lectures should be used as a way of structuring work and notes.

c. Highlight what lecturers place emphasis on when making notes.

2. Seminars

Seminars are also known as tutorials or workshops. Seminars are for sharing ideas; it is not an additional lecture! However, attendance is necessary for a comprehensive understanding of the course.

6
Finances

A t the time of writing the financial resources information provided is correct. However, as a result of Government cuts some of the financial resources referred to in this book may no longer be available. Feel free to conduct your own research for further financial assistance.

Going to university is costly. Some people have their tuition fees paid for them by their parents or a scholarship, but others need further financial assistance. This section is designed to help give an understanding of how financial help can be received to fund studies.

Jargon

Tuition fees:
The cost of the course.

Loan:
A loan is a financial transaction where the lender (eg. the student loan company) agrees to give the borrower (eg. a student) a certain amount of money with the expectation of getting all the money repaid.

Student Loans Company (SLC):
The SLC provides loans for students. These loans are paid back once the course has ended and the students have started earning a certain amount of money.

See www.slc.co.uk for more information.

My advice is to know how much the fees are likely to be, know the interest rate that will be expected to be paid and, know when and how the loan is to be paid back.

Bursaries and Awards:

A grant is given to an individual on application when they satisfy certain criteria. For more information speak with an adviser at your university student finance department.

Grants:

Financial support that does not have to be paid back.

To discover whether or not you are eligible for a grant look at the following (this list is not exhaustive):

- For frequently asked questions on student finance see http://www.offa.org.uk/students/frequently-asked-questions/
- The Educational Grants Advisory Service (EGAS) website. (http://www.family-action.org.uk/section.aspx?id=1037)
- Ask an adviser at your university careers department
- Look at publications in libraries such as:
    - Directory of Grant Making Trusts
    - Educational Grants Directory
    - Charities Digest
    - Grants Register
- The aim higher website. http://www.aimhigher.ac.uk/Uni4me/home/index.cfm. Click on "what will it cost" then "is there other

money available to help me".

This website informs you about a number of grants such as:

- Hardship Fund and Hardship loans
- University Bursaries, Grants and Sponsorships
- Access Funds and Access Bursaries
- Travel, Books and Equipment Grant
- Disabled Students Allowances (DSAs)
- Childcare Grant
- School Meals Grant
- Looked After Children
- Open University fees
- Accommodation

List taken from Aim Higher website 2011

- Another helpful website is www.unigrants.co.uk

Ways to Save Money

Create a budget

This is a good way of being financially responsible. This will help in knowing what money is being spent and identify where money is going. For an example of how to create a budget see "Appendix A" at the back of the book.

NUS card

This card grants student discounts for things such as clothing and dining. http://www.nus.org.uk

Student Beans

Many student offers are available with the aim of saving you money. http://www.studentbeans.com

Making Extra Money

If there is spare time get a part time job:
- Ask friends and family if they know of any vacancies.
- Search your student union or careers service vacancies.
- Use online websites such as www.reed.co.uk
- Be entrepreneurial and use your interests to make money, (such as, tutoring or singing at gigs).

  http://www.businesslink.gov.uk

7
Student Life

T his is a compilation of quotes from real students about their experiences at university.

CAMPUS LIFE AND GENERAL ADVICE FROM STUDENTS

Niché Bragahi,
English & French Student

Did you live on campus? No

Positive points about staying at home:
- No need to stress over rent and utility bills.
- Personal space and comfort.
- Support of family at hand.

Negative points about staying at home:
- It was harder to be involved in extracurricular activities in and around campus.
- Commuting - this took up quite a bit of my day and was physically draining.
- Less time available to make use of university resources.

Advice to prospective students:

You must take it upon yourself to understand and research all the topics dealt with and assimilate all the information. The workload is much greater than that of school/college - the onus is definitely on the student to learn for him/herself.

Belinda K. Zhawi,
Politics Student

Did you live on campus? No

Positive points about staying at home:
- I saved a lot of money.
- My life outside university continued.
- I was with my family (even though they annoyed the hell out of me).

Negative points about staying at home:
- Every time I went to university I had to travel for at least two hours.
- I didn't make full use of the library because I always had to leave at a certain time to make it home at a reasonable hour.
- I wasn't very involved in all the university activity because I wasn't there.

Advice to prospective students:

Make sure you do whatever work you have to do so you can party all you want. You don't want to be doing it two days before it is due and find yourself walking around with red eyes from a lack of sleep (I should have given myself this advice).

Sam Donaldson,
Law Student

Did you live on campus? Yes

Positive points about campus life:
- I met new people.
- I made my best university friends in halls.
- A certain night club.

Negative points about campus life:
- Constant fire alarms in halls of residence.

What you wish you were told before entering university:
- The volume of work to expect.

Advice to prospective students:
Travel for a year.

Orestis Kasinopoulos,
Psychology student

Did you live on campus? Yes

Positive points about campus life:
- You become much more independent.
- You can stay out as late as you want.
- Meeting new people from different cultures and interacting with them.

Negative points about campus life:
- Missing your mum's food.
- I am a student from outside the UK, therefore I don't have the luxury of my car.
- Not seeing your friends and family as much as you want to.

What you wish you were told before entering university:
Push yourself to the limit but enjoy and love what you are studying.

Advice to prospective students:
PARTY HARD and WORK HARD! Be open to new things as these are the best and most memorable years of your life. Try to make as many friends and connections as you can- even with staff and lecturers. Most importantly be organised and have good time management.

COMMENTS FROM GRADUATES

Sotonye Diri

What degree did you study?

At university I studied law, LLB

What are you currently doing now and why?

I am a young entrepreneur, I am a motivational speaker, I do events management, I'm trying to start up a clerking agency for university students and I'm starting up two other projects also.

The reason I have chosen this route is because to become financially free in life you need to have your eggs in more than one basket. My main career is the motivational one where I go into schools and colleges and do workshops with them. My passion is young people. Maybe later on I will go on to do law.

Is there any advice you have for prospective university students?

My advice is to follow your heart and passion. Don't chase money, chase your dream and money will come. Enjoy life by doing what you love, that's what living is about. Don't be afraid to take risks, but step out in faith. Make wise decisions and follow them through. Be flexible in case the wind changes direction. Only you can make things happen, so take full responsibility.

63

Christine Phillips

What degree did you study?

BA (honours) in Media and Video Production

What are you doing now?

I am currently making a career change and this is because being in the media industry has not been a bed of roses!

Is there any advice you have for prospective university students?

Take your time to decide what YOU want to do... mummy, daddy and Uncle Sam will not be on the job with you! It's not all about money... it's about being happy...

Final Comments

I followed the tips in this book myself to discover whether or not they worked. I went from a 3rd class degree in my first year, to a 2.1 grade in my final year.

I hope this book has given you a better understanding of university life. For more information and to give feedback on this book please visit:

www.crystaldebrah.com

Appendix

Money is something many people worry about. However, there is no need to worry if you have your spending under control. Managing your finances is a skill you need for life therefore it is beneficial to grasp the concept now.

It is vital that you know how much money you have coming in and how much is going out. It is likely you will need to adjust your budget as spending patterns change throughout the year. Ensure you do not have more going out than coming in.

Use the tables below as a guide to help you manage your finances. My advice is to create your own tables, print them out, and use them every month.

Income table (monthly)

Income	Amount (£)	
Student Loan[1]		
Bursary[2]		
Net salary[3]		
Money from parents		
	Total	

[1] Student loans come in instalments. See your letter from the Student Loan Company as it has a record of how your loan instalments will be divided. Then divide your instalments into what you will spend each month.

[2] Divide the amount you are given into what you will spend each month.

[3] "Net salary" is how much received from your job once tax has been deducted.

Outgoings (monthly)

Outgoings	Amount(£)
Rent	
Electricity	
Gas	
Food	
Travel	
Mobile phone	
Internet	
TV license	
Study materials	
Clothes	
Going out	
Gym membership	
	Total

If you are really struggling with your finances visit your university counselling service. They will point you in the right direction for further assistance.

About Crystal Debrah

Crystal Debrah has a passion for helping others. She has consistently, since the age of 16, undertaken voluntary legal work to benefit her community. Alongside pursuing a career in law Crystal has worked on projects and strategies to improve the lives of young people with organisations such as, Government Office for London and Greater London Authority. Her ambition is to use her legal, writing and interpersonal skills to make a real difference in this nation. This book is only the beginning.

Crystal is a law graduate and gained a LLB degree from the University of London (Queen Mary, University of London).

Notes

Notes

Notes

Notes

Notes